Making
paper boats

Duy Nguyen

STERLING INNOVATION
An imprint of Sterling Publishing Co., Inc.

New York / London
www.sterlingpublishing.com

STERLING, the distinctive Sterling logo, STERLING INNOVATION, and the Sterling Innovation logo are registered trademarks of Sterling Publishing Co., Inc.

10 9 8 7 6 5 4 3 2 1

Published by Sterling Publishing Co., Inc.
387 Park Avenue South, New York, NY 10016
© 2010 by Duy Nguyen

Distributed in Canada by Sterling Publishing
c/o Canadian Manda Group, 165 Dufferin Street
Toronto, Ontario, Canada M6K 3H6
Distributed in the United Kingdom by GMC Distribution Services
Castle Place, 166 High Street, Lewes, East Sussex, England BN7 1XU
Distributed in Australia by Capricorn Link (Australia) Pty. Ltd.
P.O. Box 704, Windsor, NSW 2756, Australia

Printed in China

Sterling ISBN 978-1-4027-7429-4

For information about custom editions, special sales, premium and corporate purchases, please contact Sterling Special Sales Department at 800-805-5489 or specialsales@sterlingpublishing.com.

Contents

BASIC INSTRUCTIONS 4

Symbols & Lines 6

Basic Folds 6

PAPER BOATS

Canoe 19

Ferry 26

Submarine 31

Catamaran 40

Fishing Boat 44

Sailboat 52

Battleship 59

Cruise Ship 67

Speedboat 76

basic instructions

Paper: The best paper to use for traditional origami is very thin, keeps a crease well, and folds flat. You can use plain white paper (good for learning), solid-color paper, or wrapping paper with a design only on one side. Be aware, though, that some kinds of paper stretch slightly, either in length or in width, while others tear easily.

We've provided some preprinted origami paper so that, when folded, your boats will have windows and other nautical elements. The project instructions will indicate when to use these patterned papers, as well as the correct positioning of the paper (face up or face down, for instance) to begin from. If a specific pattern is not identified for a step, then use any of the solid colors we've also included in this kit.

Wax Stick: We've included a wax stick so that you can make the paper for your boats water resistant. It's simple—just rub the wax onto the areas indicated in the project instructions. Once the paper is folded, the wax-coated part of the paper should make up the bottom and sides of your boat. For extra water resistance, rub the wax over the entire sheet of paper, and, if you run out of wax, you can find more at your local arts and crafts store. (Note: the completed cruise ship included in this kit has not been waxed.)

Glue: Use a good, easy-flowing (not loose) paper glue, but use it sparingly. You don't want to soak the paper. A flat toothpick makes a good applicator. Apply glue as needed, then allow the glued form time to dry. Avoid using stick glue, as the application pressure needed (especially if the stick has become dry) can damage your figure.

Technique: Fold with care. Position the paper, especially at corners, precisely and see that edges line up before creasing a fold. Once you are sure of the fold, use a fingernail to make a clean, flat crease. Don't get discouraged with your first efforts. In time, what your mind can create, your fingers can fashion.

Symbols & Lines

– – –	VALLEY FOLD	TURN OVER OR ROTATE
–·–·–	MOUNTAIN FOLD	FOLD AND UNFOLD
———	CREASE LINE	PLEAT FOLD
+++++++	CUT LINE	FOLD
	SCALE UP	

Basic Folds

VALLEY FOLD

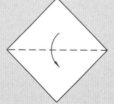

1. Fold forward.

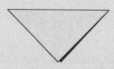

2. This is a valley fold.

MOUNTAIN FOLD

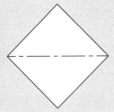 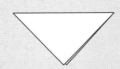

1. Fold behind.

2. This is a mountain fold.

KITE FOLD

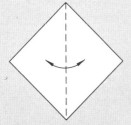 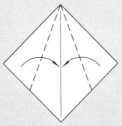 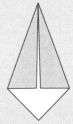

1. Fold and unfold a square diagonally, making a center crease.

2. Valley fold both sides toward the center crease.

3. This is a kite fold.

INSIDE REVERSE FOLD

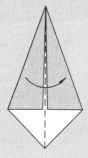

1. Start with a kite form. Valley fold.

2. Valley fold and unfold.

3. Pull tip in direction of arrow.

4. Appearance before completion.

5. This is an inside reverse fold.

OUTSIDE REVERSE FOLD

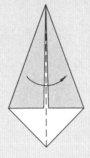

1. Start with a kite form.
Valley fold.

2. Valley fold
and unfold.

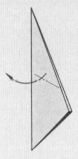

3. Fold inside out,
as shown by arrow.

4. Appearance
before completion.

5. This is an outside
reverse fold.

PLEAT FOLD

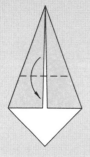  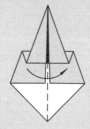 

1. Start with a kite form and valley fold.

2. Valley fold back again.

3. This is a pleat. Valley fold in half.

4. This is a pleat fold.

PLEAT FOLD REVERSE

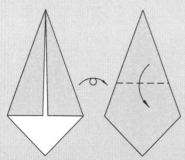 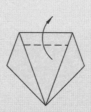 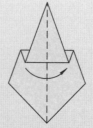 

1. Start with a kite form. Turn over.

2. Valley fold.

3. Valley fold back again for pleat.

4. Valley fold.

5. This is a pleat fold reverse.

SINK FOLD

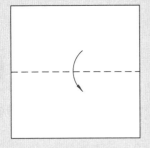

1. Valley fold.

2. Valley fold and unfold.

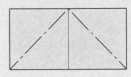

3. Inside reverse folds.

4. Valley fold and unfold.

5. Mountain fold and unfold.

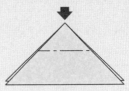

6. Push inward.

7. Appearance before completion.

8. This is a sink fold.

SQUASH FOLD I

1. Starting with a folded kite form, inside reverse fold.

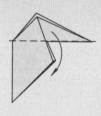

2. Valley fold.

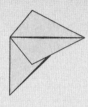

3. This is a squash fold I.

SQUASH FOLD II

1. Starting with a closed kite form, valley fold.

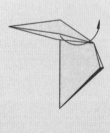

2. Pull and flatten.

3. This is a squash fold II.

INSIDE CRIMP FOLD

1. Start with a pleat fold. Pull the tip forward and fold.

2. This is an inside crimp fold.

OUTSIDE CRIMP FOLD

1. Start with a pleat fold and unfold.

2. Fold mountain and valley as shown, both sides.

3. This is an outside crimp fold.

BASE FOLD I

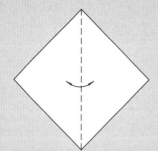

1. Valley fold and unfold.

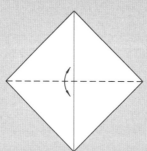

2. Valley fold and unfold.

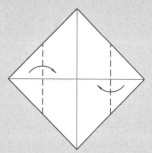

3. Valley folds.

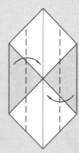

4. Valley folds.

5. Mountain fold.

6. Inside reverse folds.

7. Squash folds.

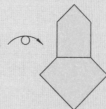

8. Turn over

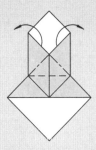

9. Squash folds.

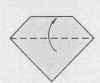

10. Valley fold.

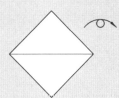

11. Turn over.

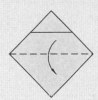

12. Valley fold.

13. Appearance before completion.

14. Valley folds.

15. Turn over.

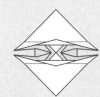

16. Valley folds and flatten.

17. Appearance before completion.

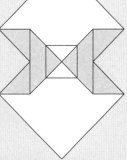

18. Completed Base Fold I.

BASE FOLD II

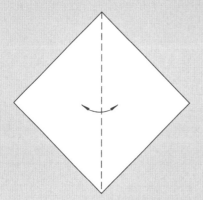

1. Valley fold and unfold.

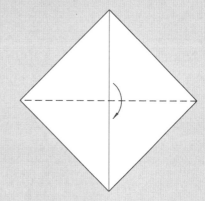

2. Valley fold.

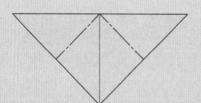

3. Inside reverse folds.

4. Valley fold and unfold both sides.

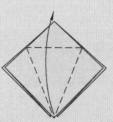

5. Valley fold and flatten.

16

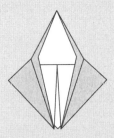

6. Appearance before completion.

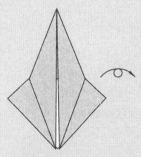

7. Turn over.

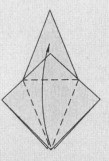

8. Repeat steps 4 and 5.

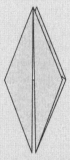

9. Completed Base Fold II.

paper boats

CANOE

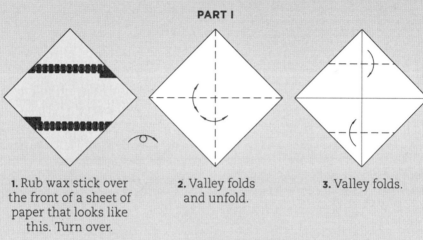

1. Rub wax stick over the front of a sheet of paper that looks like this. Turn over.

2. Valley folds and unfold.

3. Valley folds.

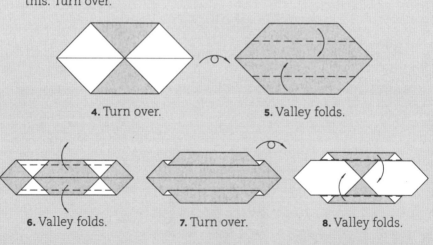

4. Turn over.

5. Valley folds.

6. Valley folds.

7. Turn over.

8. Valley folds.

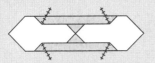

9. Cut only on the front layer.

10. Valley fold in half.

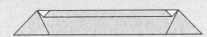

11. Inside reverse folds.

12. Cut as shown.

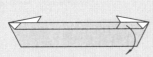

13. Unfold cut part.

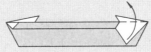

14. Valley fold.

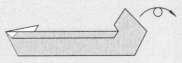

15. Turn over.

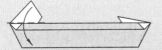

16. Valley fold.

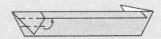

17. Mountain folds and hide under layer.

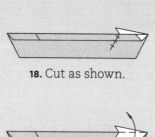

18. Cut as shown.

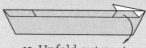

19. Unfold cut part.

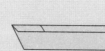

20. Valley fold.

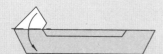

21. Turn over.

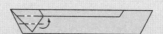

22. Valley fold.

23. Mountain folds and hide under layer.

24. Pull to open.

25. Completed Part I.

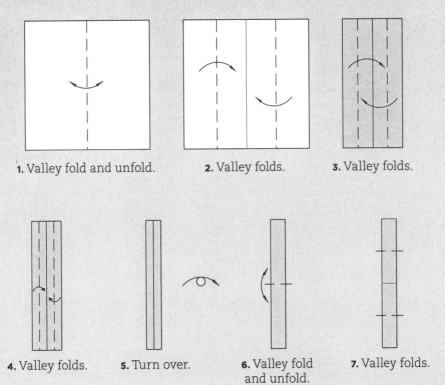

1. Valley fold and unfold.

2. Valley folds.

3. Valley folds.

4. Valley folds.

5. Turn over.

6. Valley fold and unfold.

7. Valley folds.

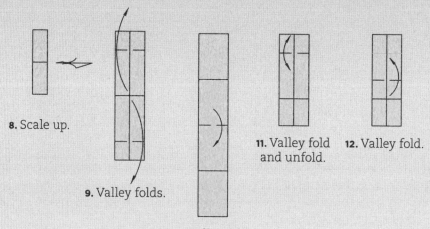

8. Scale up.

9. Valley folds.

10. Valley fold.

11. Valley fold and unfold.

12. Valley fold.

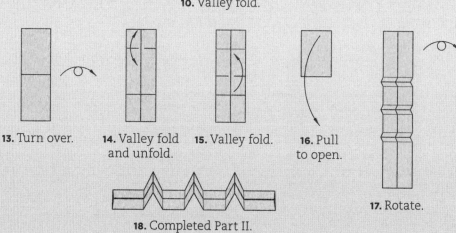

13. Turn over.

14. Valley fold and unfold.

15. Valley fold.

16. Pull to open.

17. Rotate.

18. Completed Part II.

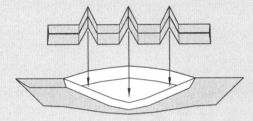

1. Insert as indicated.

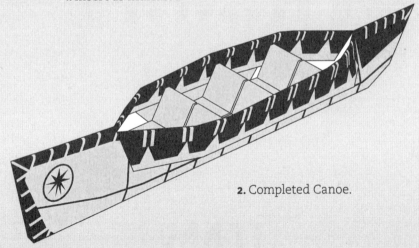

2. Completed Canoe.

FERRY

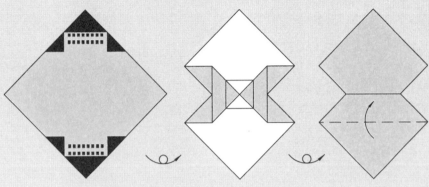

1. Start with a sheet of paper that looks like this. Turn over.

2. Create a Base Fold I. Turn over.

3. Valley fold.

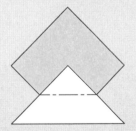

4. Mountain fold.

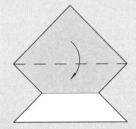

5. Valley fold.

6. Mountain fold.

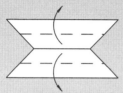

7. Valley folds with both layers.

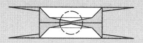

8. Glue tips together.

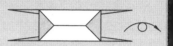

9. Rotate to side view.

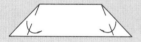

10. Valley folds.

11. Turn over.

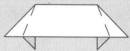

12. Valley folds.

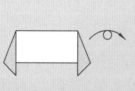

13. Rotate.

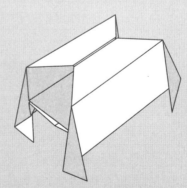

14. Completed Part I.

PART II

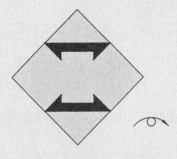

1. Rub wax over the front of a sheet of paper that looks like this. Turn over.

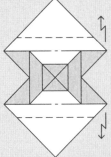

2. Create a Base Fold I. Pleat folds.

3. Valley folds.

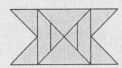

4. Tuck behind.

5. Turn over.

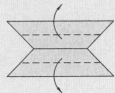

6. Valley folds to open flaps.

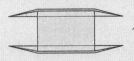

7. Turn over.

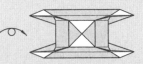

8. Completed Part II.

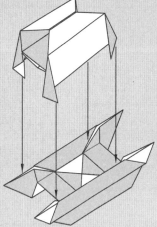

1. Insert as indicated.

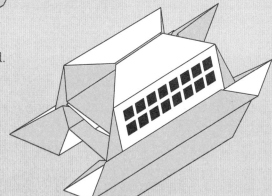

2. Completed Ferry.

SUBMARINE

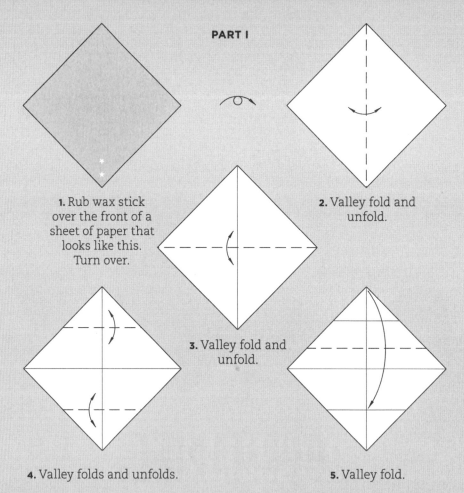

PART I

1. Rub wax stick over the front of a sheet of paper that looks like this. Turn over.

2. Valley fold and unfold.

3. Valley fold and unfold.

4. Valley folds and unfolds.

5. Valley fold.

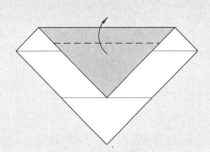

6. Valley fold.

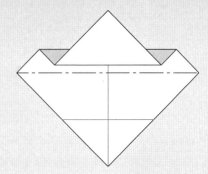

7. Mountain fold.

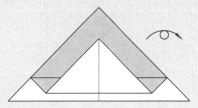

8. Turn over.

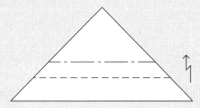

9. Pleat fold reverse.

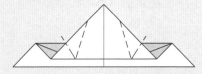

10. Squash folds on front and back.

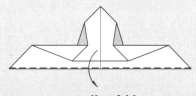

11. Valley fold.

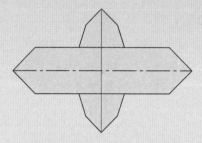

12. Mountain fold.

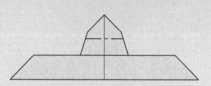

13. Mountain fold the front layer.

14. Valley fold the back layer.

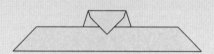

15. Hide behind the front layer.

16. Inside reverse fold.

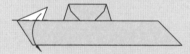

17. Valley fold.

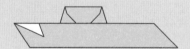

18. Hide behind the front layer.

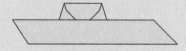

19. Completed Part I.

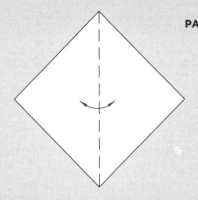

1. Rub wax stick over the front and back of a sheet of paper. Turn it over so that the back is facing up. Valley fold and unfold.

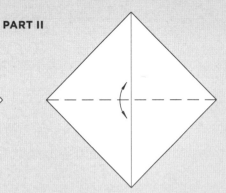

2. Valley fold and unfold.

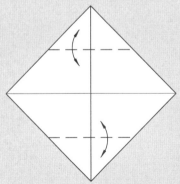

3. Valley folds and unfolds.

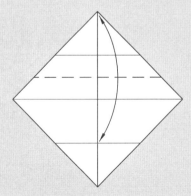

4. Valley fold and unfold.

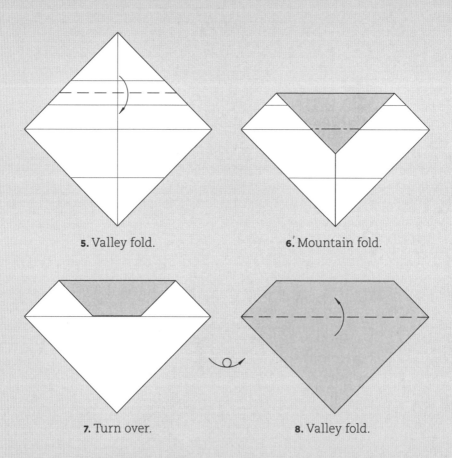

5. Valley fold.

6. Mountain fold.

7. Turn over.

8. Valley fold.

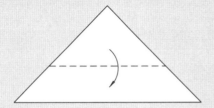

9. Valley fold.

10. Mountain fold.

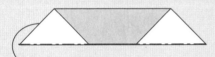

11. Mountain fold.

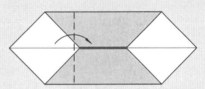

12. Valley fold.

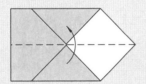

13. Valley fold.

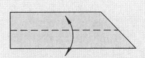

14. Valley fold and unfold.

15. Inside reverse fold.

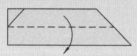

16. Valley fold.

17. Mountain fold.

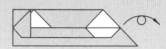

18. Turn over.

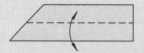

19. Valley fold and unfold.

20. Inside reverse fold.

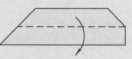

21. Valley fold.

22. Mountain fold.

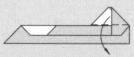

23. Valley fold.

24. Turn over.

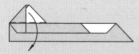

25. Valley fold.

26. Partially unfold mountain folds on the front and the back.

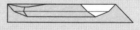

27. Completed Part II.

ASSEMBLY

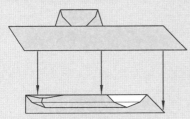

1. Insert as indicated.

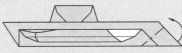

2. Inside reverse fold.

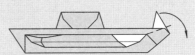

3. Inside reverse fold.

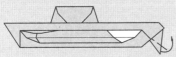

4. Inside reverse fold.

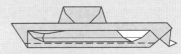

5. Valley fold.

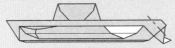

6. Mountain fold the front layer.

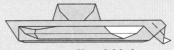

7. Valley fold the back layer.

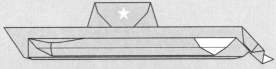

8. Completed Submarine.

CATAMARAN

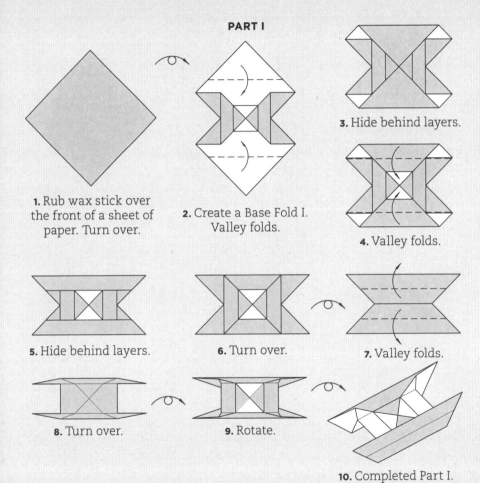

PART I

1. Rub wax stick over the front of a sheet of paper. Turn over.

2. Create a Base Fold I. Valley folds.

3. Hide behind layers.

4. Valley folds.

5. Hide behind layers.

6. Turn over.

7. Valley folds.

8. Turn over.

9. Rotate.

10. Completed Part I.

41

PART II

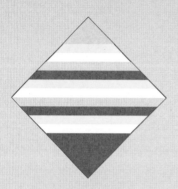

1. Start with a sheet of paper that looks like this.

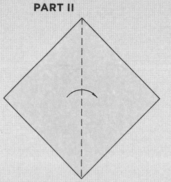

2. Valley fold.

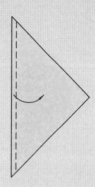

3. Valley fold.

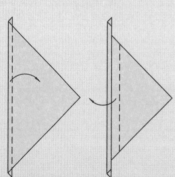

4. Valley fold.

5. Valley fold top layer.

6. Valley fold.

7. Pull in the direction of the arrow.

8. Tuck behind layer and apply glue to hold.

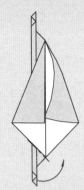

9. Inside reverse fold.

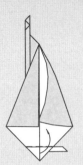

10. Valley fold top layer.

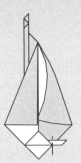

11. Mountain fold.

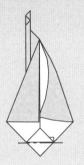

12. Mountain fold.

13. Completed Part II.

ASSEMBLY

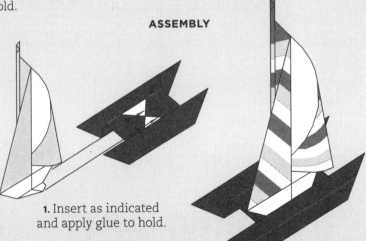

1. Insert as indicated and apply glue to hold.

2. Completed Catamaran.

FISHING BOAT

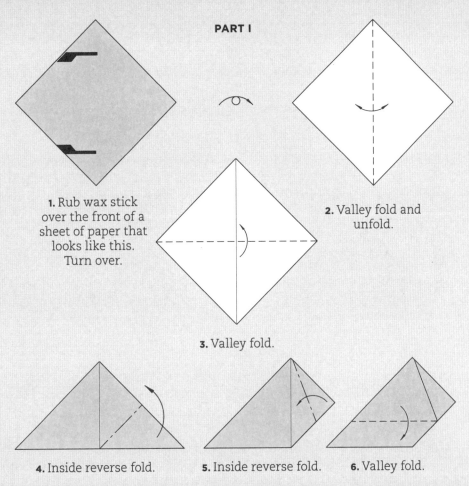

PART I

1. Rub wax stick over the front of a sheet of paper that looks like this. Turn over.

2. Valley fold and unfold.

3. Valley fold.

4. Inside reverse fold.

5. Inside reverse fold.

6. Valley fold.

45

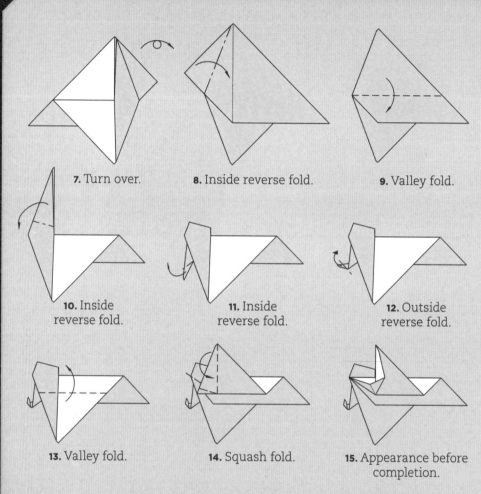

7. Turn over.

8. Inside reverse fold.

9. Valley fold.

10. Inside reverse fold.

11. Inside reverse fold.

12. Outside reverse fold.

13. Valley fold.

14. Squash fold.

15. Appearance before completion.

46

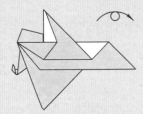

16. Turn over.

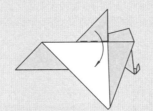

17. Valley fold.

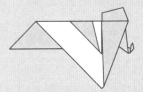

18. Hide behind layer.

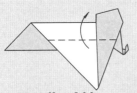

19. Valley fold.

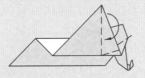

20. Squash fold.

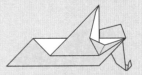

21. Appearance before completion.

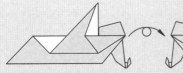

22. Turn over.

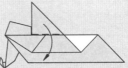

23. Valley fold.

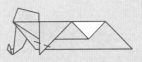

24. Valley fold.

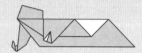

25. Hide behind layer.

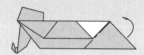

26. Inside reverse fold.

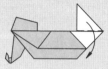

27. Valley fold.

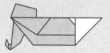

28. Hide behind layer.

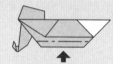

29. Sink fold.

30. Pull to open.

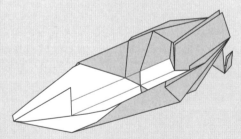

31. Completed Part I.

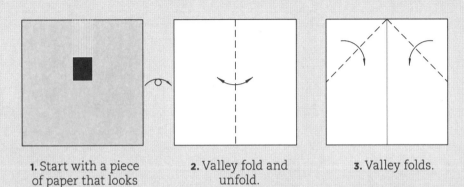

1. Start with a piece of paper that looks like this. Turn over.

2. Valley fold and unfold.

3. Valley folds.

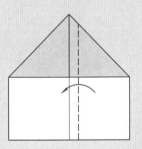

4. Valley fold.

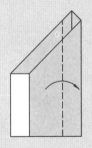

5. Valley fold top layer.

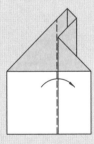

6. Valley fold.

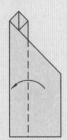

7. Valley fold top layer.

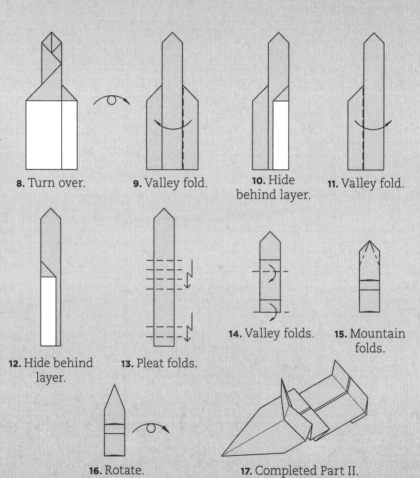

8. Turn over.

9. Valley fold.

10. Hide behind layer.

11. Valley fold.

12. Hide behind layer.

13. Pleat folds.

14. Valley folds.

15. Mountain folds.

16. Rotate.

17. Completed Part II.

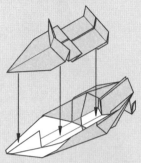

1. Insert as indicated and apply glue to hold.

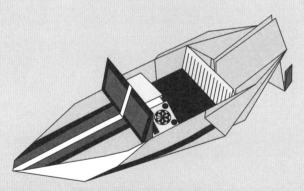

2. Completed Fishing Boat.

SAILBOAT

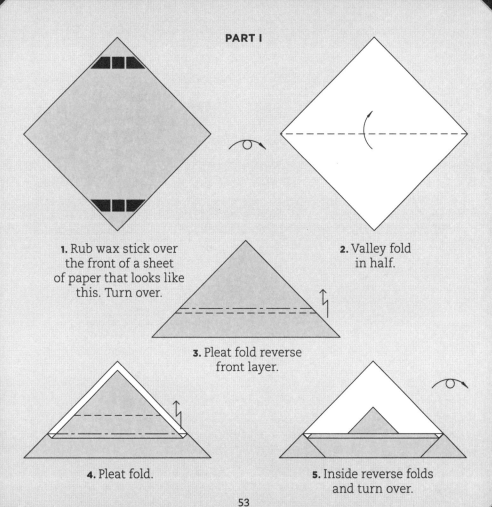

PART I

1. Rub wax stick over the front of a sheet of paper that looks like this. Turn over.

2. Valley fold in half.

3. Pleat fold reverse front layer.

4. Pleat fold.

5. Inside reverse folds and turn over.

53

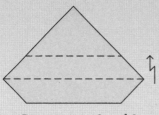
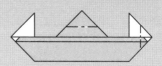

6. Repeat steps 2 and 3.

7. Mountain folds.

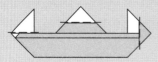
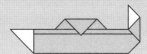
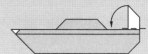

8. Valley folds.

9. Hide behind.

10. Outside reverse fold.

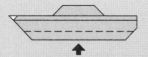
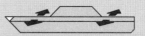

11. Sink fold.

12. Pull to open.

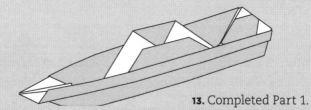

13. Completed Part 1.

PART II

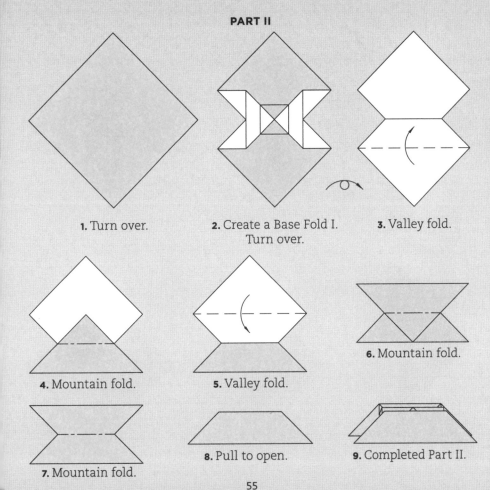

1. Turn over.

2. Create a Base Fold I. Turn over.

3. Valley fold.

4. Mountain fold.

5. Valley fold.

6. Mountain fold.

7. Mountain fold.

8. Pull to open.

9. Completed Part II.

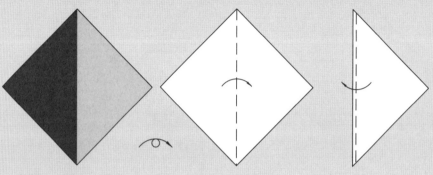

1. Start with a sheet of paper that looks like this. Turn over.

2. Valley fold.

3. Valley fold top layer.

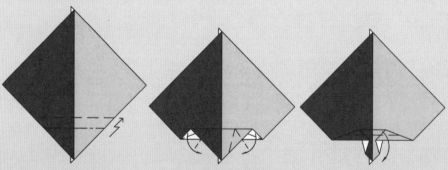

4. Pleat fold reverse.

5. Squash folds.

6. Valley fold.

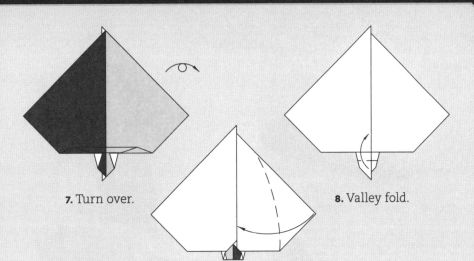

7. Turn over.

8. Valley fold.

9. Tuck behind layer and apply glue to hold.

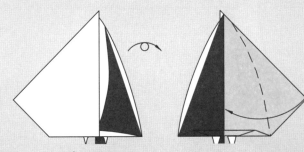

10. Turn over.

11. Tuck behind layer and apply glue to hold.

12. Completed Part III.

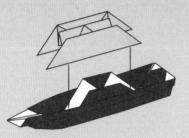

1. Insert as indicated.

2. Attach to center and apply glue to hold.

3. Completed Sailboat.

US-101
101
101

BATTLESHIP

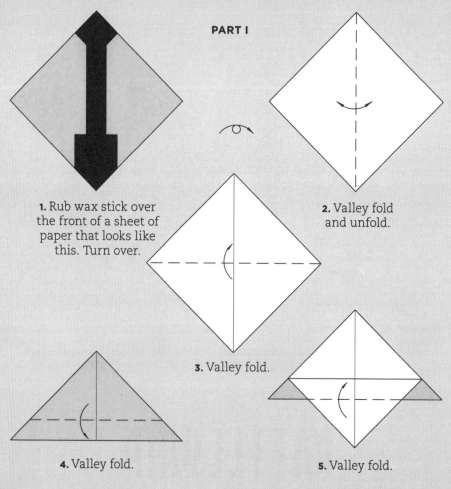

1. Rub wax stick over the front of a sheet of paper that looks like this. Turn over.

2. Valley fold and unfold.

3. Valley fold.

4. Valley fold.

5. Valley fold.

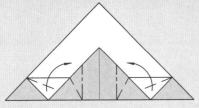

6. Squash folds.

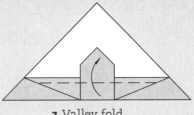

7. Valley fold.

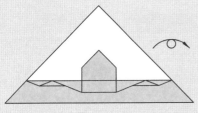

8. Turn over.

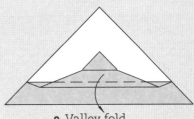

9. Valley fold.

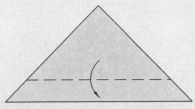

10. Valley fold.

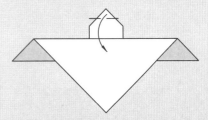

11. Valley fold.

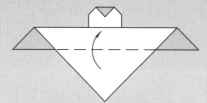

12. Valley fold.

13. Squash folds.

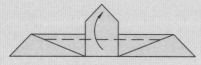

14. Valley fold.

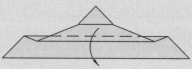

15. Valley fold.

16. Inside reverse folds.

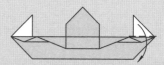

17. Valley fold.

18. Hide behind layer.

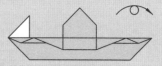

19. Turn over.

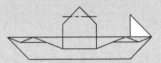

20. Mountain fold.

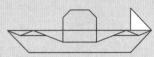

21. Repeat steps 16 and 17.

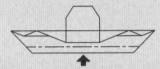

22. Sink fold.

23. Pull to open.

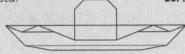

24. Completed Part I.

PART II

1. Use a sheet of paper that looks like this. Turn over.

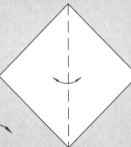

2. Valley fold and unfold.

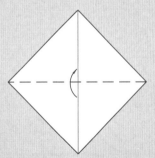

3. Valley fold.

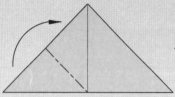

4. Inside reverse fold.

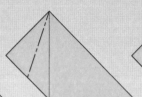

5. Inside reverse fold.

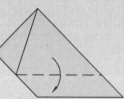

6. Valley fold.

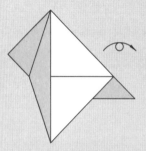

7. Turn over.

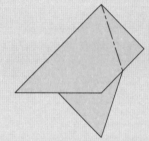

8. Inside reverse fold.

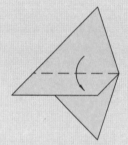

9. Valley fold.

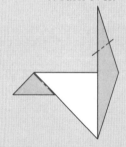

10. Inside reverse folds.

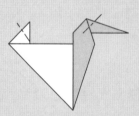

11. Inside reverse folds.

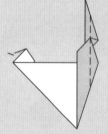

12. Valley fold to front and back.

64

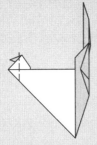

13. Mountain fold.

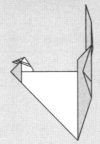

14. Pleat fold.

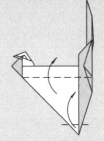

15. Valley folds to front and back.

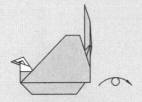

16. Turn over.

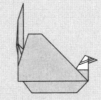

17. Pleat fold.

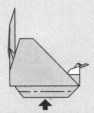

18. Sink fold.

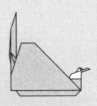

19. Completed Part II.

ASSEMBLY

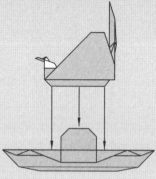

1. Insert as indicated and apply glue to hold.

2. Completed Battleship.

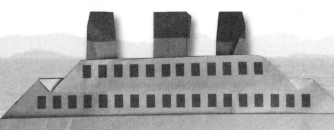

CRUISE SHIP

PART I

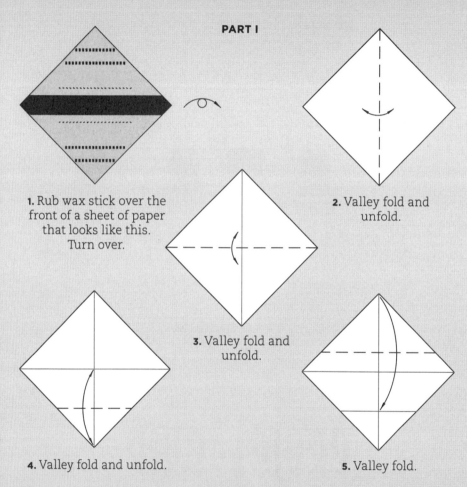

1. Rub wax stick over the front of a sheet of paper that looks like this. Turn over.

2. Valley fold and unfold.

3. Valley fold and unfold.

4. Valley fold and unfold.

5. Valley fold.

68

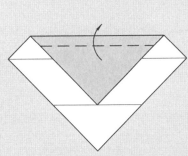

6. Valley fold.

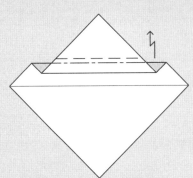

7. Pleat fold.

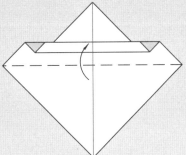

8. Valley fold.

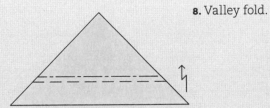

9. Pleat fold reverse.

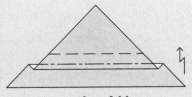

10. Pleat fold.

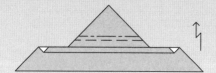

11. Pleat fold reverse.

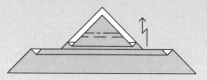

12. Pleat fold reverse.

13. Mountain fold.

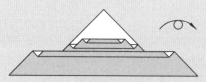

14. Turn over.

15. Pleat fold reverse.

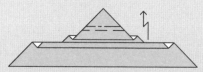

16. Pleat fold reverse.

17. Mountain fold.

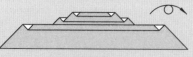

18. Turn over.

19. Hide behind layer.

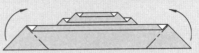

20. Inside reverse folds.

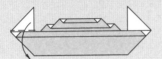

21. Valley fold.

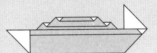

22. Hide behind layer.

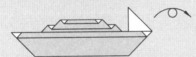

23. Turn over.

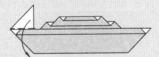

24. Valley fold.

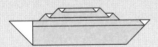

25. Hide behind layer.

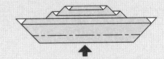

26. Sink fold.

27. Pull to open.

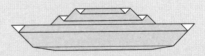

28. Completed Part I.

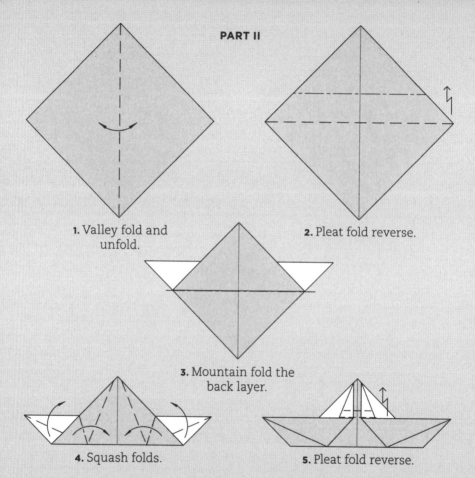

PART II

1. Valley fold and unfold.

2. Pleat fold reverse.

3. Mountain fold the back layer.

4. Squash folds.

5. Pleat fold reverse.

72

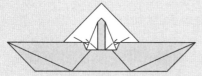

6. Reverse squash folds.

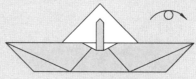

7. Turn over.

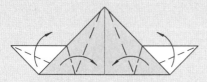

8. Repeat steps 4 to 7.

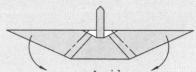

9. Inside reverse folds.

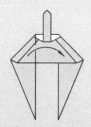

10. Valley fold.

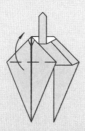

11. Valley fold.

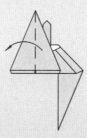

12. Valley fold.

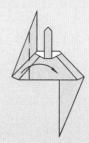

13. Valley fold.

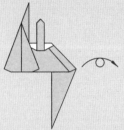 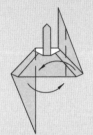

14. Turn over. **15.** Valley folds. **16.** Valley fold. 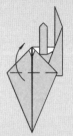  **17.** Valley fold.

 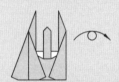

18. Valley fold. **19.** Turn over. **20.** Valley fold. **21.** Inside reverse folds.

22. Mountain fold both sides. **23.** Completed Part II.

ASSEMBLY

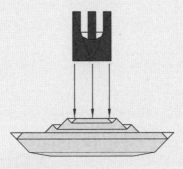

1. Insert as indicated and apply glue to hold.

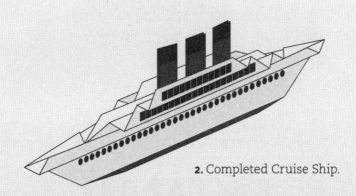

2. Completed Cruise Ship.

SPEEDBOAT

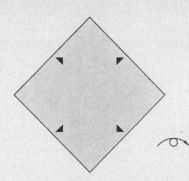

1. Rub wax stick over the front of a sheet of paper that looks like this. Turn over.

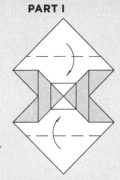

2. Create a Base Fold I. Valley folds.

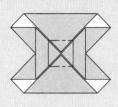

3. Mountain folds.

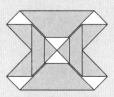

4. Turn over.

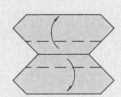

5. Valley folds.

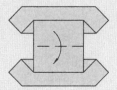

6. Valley fold.

7. Valley fold.

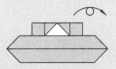

8. Turn over.

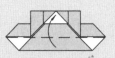

9. Valley fold.

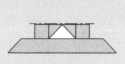

10. Mountain fold.

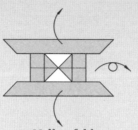

11. Valley folds and rotate.

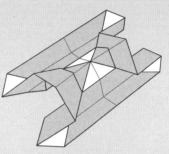

12. Completed Part I.

PART II

1. Rub wax stick over the front of a sheet of paper that looks like this. Turn over.

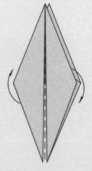

2. Make a Base Fold II. Valley fold top right layer and mountain fold back left layer.

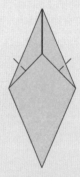

3. Inside reverse folds.

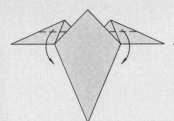

4. Valley folds.

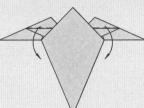

5. Valley folds and hide behind layers.

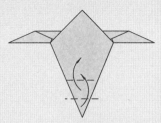

6. Valley folds.

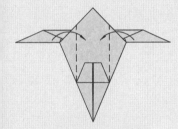

7. Valley folds and insert one side into the other.

8. Appearance before completion.

9. Completed Part II.

ASSEMBLY

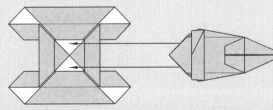

1. Place Part I on top of Part II as indicated.

79

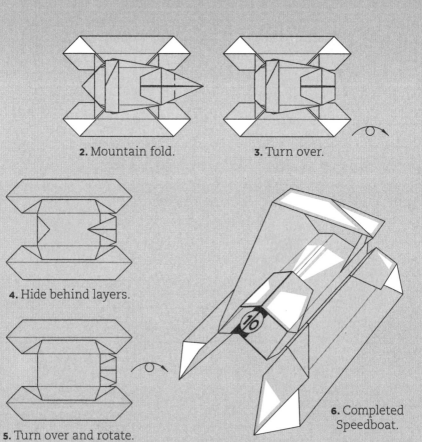

2. Mountain fold.

3. Turn over.

4. Hide behind layers.

5. Turn over and rotate.

6. Completed Speedboat.